What tools do we use...?

At home

Vic Parker

Heinemann
LIBRARY

Little Nippers

www.heinemann.co.uk/library
Visit our website to find out more information about **Heinemann Library** books.

To order:
☎ Phone 44 (0) 1865 888066
▤ Send a fax to 44 (0) 1865 314091
▭ Visit the Heinemann Bookshop at www.heinemann.co.uk/library to browse our catalogue and order online.

First published in Great Britain by Heinemann Library, Halley Court, Jordan Hill, Oxford OX2 8EJ, part of Harcourt Education.
Heinemann is a registered trademark of Harcourt Education Ltd.

Editorial: Jilly Attwood and Louise Galpine
Design: Jo Hinton-Malivoire and bigtop, Bicester, UK
Models made by: Jo Brooker
Picture Research: Rosie Garai
Production: Séverine Ribierre

Originated by Dot Gradations
Printed and bound in China by South China Printing Company

ISBN 0 431 17150 5 (hardback)
07 06 05 04 03
10 9 8 7 6 5 4 3 2 1

ISBN 0 431 17155 6 (paperback)
07 06 05 04 03
10 9 8 7 6 5 4 3 2 1

British Library Cataloguing in Publication Data
Parker, Vic
What tools do we use ...? At home
643
A full catalogue record for this book is available from the British Library.

Acknowledgements
The publishers would like to thank the following for permission to reproduce photographs: Corbis p.8; DIY Photo Library pp.**14/15, 16**; Gareth Boden pp. **4, 5, 9, 10, 11, 12, 13, 18, 19, 20/21, 22/23**; Getty Images p.6; Greg Evans p.**17** (Greg Balfour Evans); Superstock p.**7** (David Lok).

Cover photograph reproduced with permission of Gareth Boden.

The publishers would like to thank Annie Davy for her assistance in the preparation of this book.

Every effort has been made to contact copyright holders of any material reproduced in this book. Any omissions will be rectified in subsequent printings if notice is given to the publishers.

Contents

Getting up

A noisy alarm clock tells you
it is time to get up and go.

comb

Which two tools make you clean and tidy?

Scrub

Scrub

Scrub

flannel

5

Mealtime tools

Knives, forks and spoons.

Chopsticks are for **munching** rice and noodles.

Cleaning tools

One of these tools cleans up **dirt**.

Can you think of a tool that sweeps?

One of these tools makes things **shiny**.

9

Washing tools

Small, squashy sponge.

Long, thin hose.

Round, deep bucket.

Small and snappy clothes pegs.

Mending tools

Oh no! This toy is broken.

What tools do we need to mend it?

A screwdriver and a screw are just the job.

Decorating tools

Have you ever used a paintbrush or a roller like these?

Building tools

A saw is for cutting wood.

Be careful!

Can you guess what he is building?

It's a playhouse!

Sewing tools

knitting needle

zip

scissors

wool

thimble

safety pins

thread

buttons

18

pins

needle

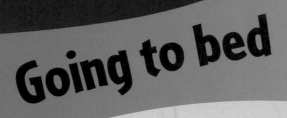

Going to bed

It's bedtime.

What tool do you use last thing at night?

What are these tools?

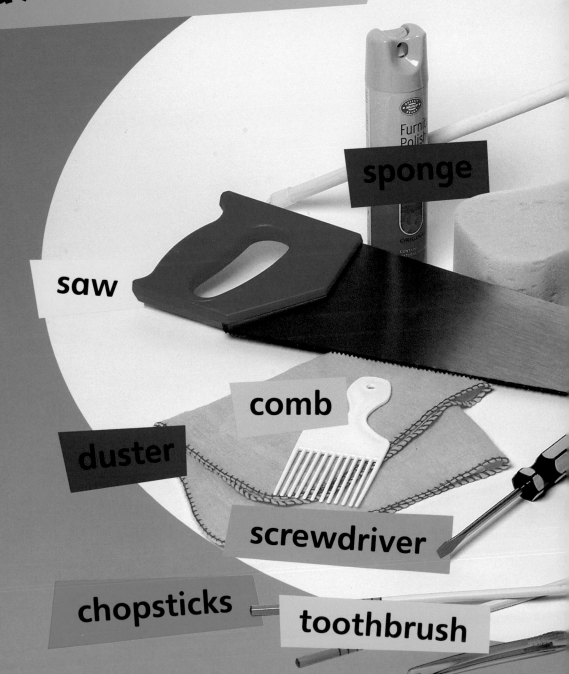

sponge

saw

comb

duster

screwdriver

chopsticks

toothbrush

feather duster

bucket

nail brush

spanner

paint brush

clothes pegs

Index

The end

Notes for adults

'What tools do we use . . .?' explores a variety of tools that a young child may come across in different situations. The series encourages young children to think creatively about the different jobs these tools do, and what other tools they might use to do the same job. The books provide opportunities for discussing how the tools should be used safely and correctly, and what materials the tools are made from. There are four titles in the series: *At school, At home, In the kitchen,* and *In the garden*. Used together, the books will enable comparison of similarities and differences between a wide variety of tools.

The key curriculum Early Learning Goals relevant to this series are:
• learn skills by using a range of tools
• select tools and techniques necessary to shape, assemble and join a range of materials
• talk about tools and their effects and how they work
• realize that tools can be used for a purpose and introduce children to appropriate tools to work on different materials
• encourage children to use the correct names for tools.

This book introduces the reader to a range of tools they may use at home. The book will help children extend their vocabulary, as they will hear new words such as *chopsticks* and *hose*. You may like to introduce and explain other new words yourself, such as *thimble* and *safety pin*.

Additional information about tools
A tool is defined as any object which you use to perform an operation to achieve an end. Tools can be small, like pencils, or large, like lawn mowers. Tools can be hand-held, such as screwdrivers, or stationary, such as pasta-making machines. Tools can be manual, like saws, or power-driven, such as hair-dryers. Tools can be classified by their function, such as: joining things or shaping things; by their mode of operation, such as: sticking things or cleaning things; or by their mode of action, such as: tools that cut, tools that mix, tools that suck.

Follow-up activities
• Draw outlines of tools such as a hammer, saw, screwdriver and spanner on some cardboard. Ask your child to identify them and colour them in.
• Cut them out and put them in an old shoebox, to make a pretend tool kit for your child.